You Got the Sugar?

Shetoya T.

DEDICATION

This book is dedicated to my team of doctors, my fellow diabetics, and those that will be affected by diabetes in the future. Most importantly it is dedicated to all those fighting for a cure.

"This is my wish for you: Comfort on difficult days, smiles when sadness intrudes, rainbows to follow the clouds, laughter to kiss your lips, sunsets to warm your heart, hugs when spirits sag, beauty for your eyes to see, friendships to brighten your being, faith so that you can believe, confidence for when you doubt, courage to know yourself, patience to accept the truth, Love to complete your life." ~ Author Unknown

CONTENTS

CHAPTER 1: DIABETES? ISN'T THAT A FAT PERSON'S DISEASE?

Her face was blank and emotionless. Amazingly, I was the one lying in the hospital bed yet my only concern was how my mother would deal with the news. After all, it seems she has always been more concerned for me than I was for myself. I knew it wasn't going to be good. There was a soft knock on the door as what seemed like a swarm of doctors entered the room.

"Ms. Russell, we got the test results back. The blood work confirms that you are a type 1 diabetic."

Wow. Now I was emotionless; perplexed. At 5'2, weighing 113lbs, I was being told I was a diabetic. Isn't that a fat person's disease?

"Ms. Russell?"

I was zoned out. Responding with a head nod I looked over to see my mother's face. Her hurt was revealing itself in the form of tears.

"...Ms. Russell we will be getting you a room as soon as possible. You need to stay for about a week or so. We understand that it is getting late. We will allow you to rest and tomorrow we will have a counselor speak with you".

I couldn't stop looking at her.

Snapping back into reality I asked, "A counselor? For what?"

The residents looked confused as if I asked a stupid question.

"Ma'am we recommend patients finding out that they have a chronic health condition speak with someone. After all, this is an issue that you will have to deal with for the rest of your life."

Forcing a smile I responded, "Could have been worse right? You could have told me I have cancer."

They all smiled. With that, the room was slowly cleared.

My mom began digging in her purse feverishly. Pulling out her cellphone and cigarettes she stood up, "I'm going to go smoke okay?"

I grinned, "Okay".

She wasn't a good liar. She was going to go cry. Lying there in silence only one thing continued to cross my mind. *Can I still eat cake?* I was willing to give up many things. But cake was not one of them. As I waited on her to return I replayed the day's events in my head to grasp how I got there. How did I end up in the hospital two weeks after my 21st birthday? How will I live the normal life of a young adult when my days would be surrounded by needle sticks and finger pricks? Does Janine even know that she saved my life?

During the summer months I was an intern at the Sheraton Chicago Hotel and Towers. It was a job that afforded me great opportunities and great money. Being a sociable person it was only natural that I enjoyed greeting people at the front desk. However, I was sleepy a lot at work. My sleepiness was attributed to my newly encountered night life as a young adult. Or so I thought. While walking to the bathroom for the millionth time that day Janine asked to see me.

"Let me check your sugar..."she asked aggressively.

Was she crazy? I was going to willingly let her prick my finger for the fun of it?

I raised my eyebrows, "Why?"

She looked serious, "Because you go to the bathroom too much and you drink too much. Every time I see you there is a bottle of water or a pop in your hand. Those are two signs of diabetes."

I shrugged and extended my finger. Pulling out a one touch meter she wiped my finger tip with alcohol, changed her lancelet, and pricked me. The meter began to countdown. 5, 4, 3, 2, 1....blood glucose? 460.

"Is that normal?" The entire room was quiet.

Janine spoke, "Absolutely not. Normal is between 80 and 120."

She sighed and continued, "Let's wait 30 minutes and check it again. Maybe something is wrong."

I nodded my head and walked away. Heading to the cafeteria I knew my fate. All I really knew about diabetes is how much people with the disease could not do. If I was going to live my life with a bunch of "No's" I was going to enjoy a few simple pleasures one last time. I grabbed my food to eat one last normal meal; a polish, some french fries, a sprite, and a piece of cake. When I finished lunch I walked back over to Janine's desk. Now I was really sleepy. I couldn't keep my eyes open at all.

Feeling as if I could sleep standing up I gave her my finger again. The meter began to count down again, 5, 4, 3, 2, 1....HIGH. No number would register on it at all. The meter doesn't go that high. The room was in a bit of an uproar. My mom was a manager in the reservations department; the department in which Janine worked. She stood up immediately.

"Go get your things we're headed to the hospital."

I did just that. Jumping in the cab I could see the worry on my mother's face. She called the troops (Granny, Auntie Nettie, Auntie Donna, Demarri, and Dre) to inform them of our whereabouts. Laying my head on her shoulder, while we rode to the hospital, all I could think about was how sleepy I was. Walking into the emergency room everything was a blur. I remember my mom telling the nurse of my problem, being placed on a bed, and being given insulin to bring down my sugar. It wasn't until moments before the doctors walked in that everything else seemed clear.

That night Northwest Memorial Hospital in Chicago admitted me. One great thing is that they do not have visiting hours or a limit to how many visitors patients can have at one time. My friend stayed overnight on the couch by the window for comfort. Comfort that was much needed and appreciated. The following morning after waking I discovered Disney themed pens and candy by my bedside that my brother had brought when he came to visit at 1:00am. A visit that I had no memory of due to the medicine that was administered prior to me falling asleep.

Breakfast was horrible that morning and I whined like the spoiled brat that I am. A small juice, a slice of toast, eggs, and sausage. Hospital food at its best. A few hours later a nurse came toting a large syringe and a bottle of a saline solution. In the sweetest tone imaginable she explained that she will be teaching me how to give myself insulin by way of a saline. After a small tutorial was given I was inserting a needle into my side with tears slowly streaming down my face. They weren't tears of pain…simply tears of life. I cried because now, two weeks after my 21st birthday, I would be living a new life.

After speaking to a "counselor", watching a video on how to live after discovering you're a type 1 diabetic, and several lessons the nurse stopped to ask, "What type of insurance do you have?"

I was a little agitated with the question. With all the paperwork, videos, and pamphlets they were giving they should at least know what kind of insurance I had.

I smirked, "A PPO ma'am." She was a plump little lady that reminded me of Mrs. Clause.

"Well, that's different! I will be right back."

She left the room and retuned shortly with a hand full of things. I would no longer use syringes. Now that they discovered I had "good insurance" I would be using insulin pens. Novolog insulin before every meal and Levemir insulin before going to sleep every night. I also got a new glucose meter. A One Touch Ultra to be exact when previously I had some meter without a name. The doctor came in to speak with me but I cut him off before a single word exited his mouth.

"When can I go home?"

"Well..." he paused, "...We normally recommend that a person stay here for roughly a week." My eyebrows scrunched up and I became a little irate.

"I'm not staying here for a week. I'm telling you that now. I want to go home. I get everything you are saying. I'm not stupid. But I am not staying here. I promise you I'm not." I began to cry.

The doctor looked frightened. "Well, let's see how tomorrow goes and you can possibly go home in two days."

I continued to cry in silence. As soon as the medical staff left the room I saw my grandfather turning beet red. Before I knew it he blew his top.

"You must be out of your got damn mind! If the doctor says that you stay your butt in here for two damn weeks then that's what the hell you're going to do. Who the hell are you to tell him different?! HE'S THE DAMN DOCTOR!"

I fell out laughing. My grandfather had never cursed me out before. It tickled me and everyone else. Needless to say within two days I was released from the hospital with a bag full of insulin pens, meters, and papers.

Walking out the hospital doors I mumbled to myself, "Now my life begins."

Lesson #1: Find Inspiration after your diagnosis

Deal with it. Deal with the fact that you will live your life under a label full of ignorance. Deal with the fact that you have to change your eating habits a little. Deal with the fact that your life will be full of needle sticks and finger pricks. Do not pretend as if you didn't just get the bad news. You have to find inspiration. Does that mean that you won't have bad days in which you feel as though nobody understands? No. To be completely honest only a fellow diabetic could truly relate. After my diagnosis I discovered five things that helped keep me inspired:

1.   Remember it could always be worse. Many days I would think about the fact that I walked into the hospital as a 'normal' person and walked out with a diabetes diagnosis. However, someone else didn't walk out the hospital at all. Someone else walked into the hospital and was told that they had one week to live. Whether it feels like it or not, it could actually be worse.

2.   Laugh until it hurts. Once while on Christmas break from college I slept in late (enjoying the fact that I didn't have class). Stretching as I walked into the kitchen I yawned a slow good morning to my parents.

My dad started in, "Are these your dishes in the sink?"

Before I could answer he finished, "wash them."

Smirking I turned around to head back into my room as I shot back, "I can't wash dishes. I'm a diabetic."

Before I knew it the entire house was laughing uncontrollably. After that day whenever I didn't want to do anything my excuse was that I'm a diabetic. It always gave people a great laugh.

3.   Surround yourself with supportive people. This speaks for itself. If your friends and family choose to poke fun at the fact that you are insulin dependent or choose to tell stories about who they know that got a limb cut off, then they are not considerate of you/your disease at all. Inform

them of their rudeness and spend more time with those that are concerned with your mental and physical well-being.

4.   Get in tuned with the diabetic community. Join support group for diabetics, an online forum, or meet a fellow diabetic at the endocrinologist. Everyone needs someone they can connect to. Everyone needs someone that understands.

5.   Live life to the fullest! Don't stop doing anything you were doing before. Rock climbing, karaoke, kick boxing, singing, dancing, dating, or whatever it is that you like to do. Your life isn't over; you just have to make some adjustments.

CHAPTER 2: LET THEM EAT CAKE!

The biggest misconception I had when I found out that I was a type 1 diabetic was thinking that I had to eliminate sweets completely in order to avoid losing a limb at some point in my life. I began seeing a diabetic educator as well as a nutritionist in order to get a grasp on my life. My diabetic educator began telling me how much easier life would be if I began to carb count. I had no clue what carb counting was. However, the more she told me the more questions I asked my nutritionist.

Once while learning about how to properly read nutrition fact labels I asked, "Can I eat cake? Because I had a piece of cake yesterday."

She smiled, "Yes, you can eat cake. The key is 'how' you eat cake."

I looked down at my feet wondering how honest I should be. Why not be honest with her? Her purpose was to teach me the proper way to do things, right?

I sighed, "Confession time."

She giggled, "Confess…"

Grinning I blurted out, "Ok, I didn't just have one piece of cake. An hour later I had another, and so on and so forth."

She didn't seem too upset. "How many carbs are in a piece of cake?"

I had no clue. Why would she ask me? I shrugged my shoulders.

She continued, "You have to learn these things Shetoya. You binged on the cake because you have eliminated everything sweet out of your life completely. You use sugar-free syrup, sugar- free jelly, etc. So when you craved a sweet yesterday and got that little taste you ultimately lost your mind," We both laughed, "The sooner you carb count the easier life will be for you and the sooner you will see that you can have many things. It's about checking your sugar, taking the appropriate amount of insulin, and not going overboard. What kind of cake was it?"

I laughed, "Red Velvet."

"Well, you have homework. Tell me how many carbs is in a slice of red velvet cake when you come back next week."

Little did I know, carb counting would mend my relationship with food. The more that I gained a better understanding about what I could eat, the more the ignorance of those around me drove me nuts. If I picked up a cookie, "You know you shouldn't have that". If I ate a scoop of ice cream, "Can you eat that?!" It never failed. Don't be fooled. I didn't have it down to a science (and still don't to tell the truth) however I managed pretty well.

Many people get it misconstrued when they think about the relationship that a diabetic has with food. It's a matter of "how" not "can". During a visit with my endocrinologist she plugged up my continuous glucose monitor to download a chart.

"Things are looking better but in the mid-morning there is a spike. What do you eat for breakfast?"

I shrugged, "Bagels, cereal, or whatever I can get my hands on."

She pointed to the chart, "That's the problem. Cereal."

She shook her finger like she always does when she disagrees with something I am saying. She turned to face me, "To be honest all cereal is bad. One cup is generally a serving. That's small. And it's all sugar. But I can help you trick your body a little. If you really want cereal then you have to take your insulin twenty minute prior. If you can't take it twenty minutes prior, don't eat it. Deal?!"

I smiled, "Deal."

All I knew is that I wanted to eat cereal. She also recommended that I start eating more protein and things such as Jimmy Dean's breakfast sandwiches (any with little sodium).

The following day I tested her theory, (like she doesn't know what she's talking about right?), and surely my blood sugar was lower before I ate lunch. I was pleased with one of the new tricks I learned. This wasn't the first trick of course. I learned years prior that in order to avoid a spike after eating pizza I have to take half of my insulin before eating and the rest halfway through my meal. Oh how I love my endocrinologist. Contrary to the opinion of many people, I eat well as a diabetic.

As time went on I learned that as much carb counting as I would do there would still have to trial and error when it came to certain food. For instance I know how much insulin I need to take when I am drinking a small vanilla shake. How do I know that? Once I didn't take enough insulin and my sugar shot through the roof. Another time I took too much and it dropped to the floor. Eventually I found the perfect medium. Now don't get it confused. I didn't try to a vanilla shake every day until I figured it out. That would have been unnecessarily stressful to my body. However, I needed to understand how certain foods affected my body; especially "sweets".

The inconvenience of being a type 1 diabetic is also the convenience; Insulin. Insulin allows type 1 diabetics to eat more "freely" as opposed to type 2's. This does not mean that food still does need to be monitored.

Once while meeting with my nutritionist I asked her, "How often can I eat sweets?"

She placed her pen down and looked at me, "How often SHOULD anyone eat sweets? No one, whether they are diabetic or not, should have a piece of cake or cookies daily. It's just not healthy. Don't eat a certain way because you're a type 1. Eat well because it is what you should be doing anyway."

That made sense. I began using that logic. I would treat myself to ice cream, cake, or cookies but I would do so in moderation. Being insulin dependent is irritating but having to use insulin at every meal is what allows me to self-correct faster. As time goes on I learned that for many years my life as a diabetic would be trial and error.

Lesson 2: Carb Counting

According to Joslin Diabetes Center, there are several benefits to carb counting:

- "Counting carbohydrates is a good solution for many people with diabetes. Once you learn how to count carbs, you'll find it easier to fit a wide variety of foods into your meal plan, including combination foods such as those in frozen dinners. For example, by checking the grams of total carbohydrate on the Nutrition Facts label on a frozen dinner, you can figure out how to fit the dinner into your carb allotment for a particular meal. Many people find carb counting to be much easier than using a more traditional exchange meal plan. "

- "Another benefit of counting carbohydrates is that it can bring tighter control over your glucose readings. Being as precise as possible with your carb intake and medication will help you better manage your blood glucose after meals."

- "Lastly, if you take mealtime insulin, counting carbohydrates allows you to decide how much carb you want to eat at a meal, rather than having to eat a certain amount of carbohydrates, even if you do not want to." http://www.joslin.org/info/Carbohydrate_Counting_101.html

Below is a chart I created upon learning how to carb count. With this chart I was able to visibly see how I was maintaining my meals and carbs during the day. This chart also allowed me to give my doctors a better insight into my diabetic life. Truthfully speaking it is not easy to remember to write down every single thing you do, and at times it is overwhelming. However, it gets better. It gets easier. It becomes a normal routine in your life.

Date:			
Meal	Total Carbs	Insulin Amount	Time
Meal	Total Carbs	Insulin Amount	Time
Meal	Total Carbs	Insulin Amount	Time

CHAPTER 3: I'M TOO CUTE FOR THAT

Carb counting was extremely beneficial although there were bumps in the road to perfect glucose management. Every time I went to visit the endocrinologist they would push an insulin pump or a continuous glucose monitor. All I could think about was that I was too cute to attach some contraption to my side. What about when I wanted to wear sexy dresses or go swimming? What about intimate moments? What about when I wanted to take a bath? I was just beginning to enjoy my twenties and I refused to allow a pump or sensor let me feel like a robot. I went to visit Dr. Klaw one day.

"Shetoya, have you thought any more about the pump?"

Was she deaf? I have told her a million times that I didn't want any of that stuff. I was fine with my insulin pens and one touch meter.

I was snappy, "There is nothing to think about. Don't want it." She was used to my smart mouth after so many years of working closely together.

"If nothing else you should attend a class that informs you about all of the devices to aide management. Do me that favor at least."

I sighed, "I can do that."

She signed me up for the course (failing to let me know that it was four hours) and I solicited my mom to go with me. When I arrived at the course I was surprising uncomfortable. Being around so many of "my kind" was rare. Before the representatives from Dexcom and Medtronic's began speaking I saw other type 1's pulling out insulin pens and administering shots while grabbing snacks. I saw people taking out glucose meters to check their sugar. I saw people eating a few crackers to raise their sugar. This in and of itself threw me for a loop seeing as though I was used to being the odd woman out.

Once the presentations began I was intrigued. There were demonstrations on how to properly hide an insulin pump no matter what you are wearing as well as the A1C (three month average of your sugar) benefits to owning a continuous glucose monitor. If nothing, they gained my interest. I submitted my paperwork and started the process of owning my own monitor. It was a bit of a lengthy process however, I was happy that I would begin a new chapter in the book of my diabetic life.

When my monitor arrived I had to meet with a nurse so that she could teach me how to change my sensor weekly. It was nerve wrecking even though I stuck myself with needles all day long. I think it was the "newness" of the device. We chatted while we let the device charges. We talked about the necessity for diabetic youth support groups as well as other things. She told me stories about young women who were feeling inadequate due to fertility issues as well as insecurities surrounded the marks the needles sometimes left. I was shocked by how little of a support system many of them had. Kim had been my nurse for many years and we had developed a great relationship. Her personality and demeanor was always comforting. Feeling like a complete idiot after she helped me put on the sensor for the first time I shrugged, "Easy huh?"

She pat my abdomen playfully, "Yes, easy." Before leaving the hospital room I took a few pictures of the monitor with my cellphone to send to family and friends. Honestly speaking I was excited. It was like having a new toy. Things went well throughout the day with the monitor. Before bed I made sure that I placed the wireless unit by my pillow so that the sensor could read it. I closed my eyes to sleep and all things…got…real. There were alerts set on the sensor. An alarm would go off when my blood sugar went below 80 or when it would rise above 220. After a peaceful hour of sleep the alarm went off. Jumping out of bed startled I checked to see what my sugar was; 240 and rising. I took a few units of insulin and lay back down to sleep. A few hours later I woke to the buzzing of the alarm again. Blood sugar was 68 and dropping. What? Drinking some juice and leaning on the refrigerator I sighed, "This is some crap."

The walk back to the bedroom seemed unnecessary. Drifting into a deep sleep on the couch I hoped I wouldn't hear the alarm anymore before the morning. As I fixed breakfast I thought about the fact that I made it through the night without hearing the alarm at all. When I walked into my bedroom to get my cellphone I realized why I hadn't heard the alarm all night. I left the wireless portion by the pillow. The screen read "Out of range". Ooops! For several hours my glucose wasn't being recorded because the sensor couldn't be read. Laughing to myself I thought about the good sleep I was able to get the last couple hours before I started work. The fact of the matter is that it was an adjustment full of mistakes and blunders. However, it was and continues to be a great addition to my life.

Lesson #3: Change is constant and progressive. Most importantly, change is necessary

The "old school" mentality of diabetes management no longer works. The world as well as the disease has changed since fifty years ago so why would you follow the original rules for maintenance? It doesn't make sense. Is it common to fear the new trials, technology, and medicine? Of course it is. However, if you as a diabetic don't take a hand on approach in fighting for a cure, how could you remotely expect anyone else to? Embody change. Take the time to learn about the changing world of diabetes. Learn about the new technology, the trials you can take part in, and the medicine that's evolving daily. Make a difference. Every year the Juvenile Diabetes Research foundation has several Walk to Cure diabetes events going on around the country. Since my diagnosis, every October I have participated with the walk supported by a team of friends and family. There is educational information provided, food, and plenty of activities for the children. Most importantly it is a chance to make a difference one way or another.

I took some time to learn about how diabetes has evolved. In the 17th century many physicians were testing for diabetes by tasting urine. People who were diabetic had a "sweeter" taste in their urine. Physicians were using flowers, almonds, and oils to "help" people who were diabetic; diabetes was a death sentence. Insulin wasn't discovered until the early 20th century. The single syringe wasn't created and introduced until the late 1970's and the A1C wasn't used as a form of measurement and maintenance until the 1990's. Like I said, change is constant and necessary.

CHAPTER 4: EXERCISE SMEXERCISE

Throughout the course of my life I have been athletic. I started running track at the age of eleven. I started playing basketball at the age of thirteen. By the time I went away to college I was burned out from the track and field/cross country life. However, I played flag football each spring in tournaments. I love sports…but I hated to exercise. Whenever I wasn't a part of organized sports I rarely exercised. I would start an exercise regimen in order to assist my friends on their plight to lose weight (I am motivated in a group setting as I alluded to before). Once while talking to my endocrinologist she asked me how often I exercised.

I smirked, "Every now and then".

She spun around in her stool, "How often is that? Numbers please? Once a week, or three times a week?"

I shrugged, "Every now and then is like whenever I feel like it. Sometimes I work out 3-4 times a week. Other times I may not work out at all for 3 weeks. It just depends."

She shook her finger as an upset grandmother would do, "Not good Shetoya. Not good."

So, I tried to start working out. I would go to the gym in my building. I would run almost every day after work. I was pretty successful with it in the beginning until everyone started talking about the amount of weight I was losing. I was already small and I didn't want to be smaller. Many clothes that were a size 4 were falling off of me. I was back to wearing a size 2. Not cool in my eyes. Someone suggested that I start taking supplements. Whey Protein became my drug of choice. Mixing it in smoothies in the morning or night seemed reasonable nevertheless, it affected my glucose. As to be expected…the exercising stopped. While speaking to a friend that worked at a gym (not too far from my home) she suggested getting a personal trainer. I received a text message from the trainer who said that he would help me eat in a manner that was healthy and would also help me to maintain weight. This in itself gained my interest. The price helped a lot as well. I was under the impression that a personal trainer would not fit into my monthly budget. It did.

The first meeting between he and I was a little intimidating. There was a weigh in as well as a conversation about what was expected. After a few weeks my semi-private workouts became more intense.

While completing my pushups one day I began, "I have noticed that the other women you train do less that I do. Why am I doing the same things your men are doing for the most part?"

He smiled, "Because I know what you can do. Back down for the pushups sunshine."

"But Zak…."

He cut me off, "Back down."

This was just what I needed. Some people are motivated enough to work out on their own. I was honest with myself. I needed to be told what to do. I looked forward to the days I worked out as well as the energy I had after a workout was complete. Every few days I sent emails detailing my meals for the day as well as the amount I ate. Maintaining weight was becoming easier.

I met with Zak twice a week. I was beginning to love the way working out made look as well feel. While working out one Tuesday morning I kept stopping due to immense pain in the back of my mouth. It was a pain so unbearable that I had to rush into the bathroom to vomit.

Zak was worried. "Did you eat breakfast Sunshine?"

I nodded a slow yes.

He sighed with concern, "We're done for the day. We will start back thursday."

Immediately I made an appointment with a dentist. For the record, I am no stranger to pain. I have ten tattoos, piercings, and thrilling adventures always find me. However, I am AFRAID of the dentist. It seems as though everything they do hurts; even the cleaning. After a short examination the dentist told me that the wisdom teeth in the back of my mouth needed to be removed. Within a week or two they were extracted. I was extremely worried about the length of time I would be hurting seeing as though as a diabetic it takes me longer to heal.

As weeks went by I was feeling like death. The dentist kept reassuring me that my mouth would heal in due time. Time progressed and I was taking enough hydrocodone to create an addiction. Needless to say a second opinion was needed. During my appointment with the oral surgeon a 3D x-ray of my mouth was taken. With a somber look on his face he began to show me the results of a bad extraction job.

"Well, I discovered what the problem is…"

I raised my eyebrows.

"…You're teeth weren't extracted. They were broken off. The roots are still in your mouth and they are actually very close to your nerves."

I generally maintained a high level of class while in professional settings but I was furious. "Unf*cking believable. So what has to happen?"

He smirked, "Well we have to put you under to remove them. But ultimately we suggest that all of your wisdom teeth are removed to avoid any problems in the future. This is why your body has been having such a hard time healing."

I was so angry. All I could think about was how my vacation in Nassau was uncomfortable a week before due to the fact that my first dentist was a barbarian. Who breaks your teeth off? I scheduled my surgery before leaving and was given antibiotics to clear up the infection that had developed in my mouth. To make matters worse the pain and stress that I was in since the beginning of this ordeal had caused my blood sugar to be completely horrible. I was consistently maintaining an average of about 280. Seeing anything under 200 was a rarity. I was furious. The surgeon informed me that I would be unable to drive afterwards so I need to have someone come with me. Thank God for my best friend Donne' who showed up with my godson in tote.

"Okay Shetoya, who is one of your favorite artists?"

I thought for a second, "Trey Songs."

The nurse scrolled through an iPod. "I have his new album. I will put that on for you."

Placing a mask over my face she continued, "Who came with you today?"

I didn't even answer the question. I giggled, "Am I supposed to feel giddy?"

Smiling she replied, "Yes. It's laughing gas. And laughing gas does have a lot of people laughing."

"What about…"

Before I could get it out she finished, "Paranoid? Yes it does that too. Now count backwards from ten." Before I knew it the operation was over.

The wounds in my mouth took months to heal. Once again I was on hydrocodone and struggling to maintain a good blood sugar average. An issue that would be over within a few weeks for other people lasted over six months for me.

Lesson #4: Find a workout regimen that works for you

1.   Consult your physician first before beginning a new workout regimen.

2.   Determine your physical/health needs. (Does your physician want you to maintain or lose weight?)

3.   Determine if you believe you can be self-motivated or if you will need an additional push. (Do you need a class, personal trainer, etc.)

4.   Determine whether you would be more comfortable working out in a personal environment (home) or if a gym would suit you better.

5.   Buy some cool workout clothes and get started! (You have to look good even though you will be sweating profusely right?)

CHAPTER 5: UNTIL YOUR PANCREAS STOPS WORKING...SHUT UP

The results of the A1C were consistently well for several months. Abruptly, that changed. Every morning the numbers seemed to be higher. Certain that it was an issue created by me I tried to self-correct before consulting a physician; an uphill battle to say the least. Finally I did what should have been done all along. I called my endocrinologist. For weeks my meals, carb intake, and insulin distribution was recorded. Did I forget to write down vital information? Of course. I wouldn't be me if I didn't. However, I collected enough data to help my doctors make an assessment.

She raised her eye brows, "Well...you're pancreas just isn't working."

She said it as if my favorite toy had run out of batteries. By now it wasn't good or bad news in my opinion when it came to my health. It was just NEWS.

"So what does that mean?"

"It means that maybe the long lasting insulin you take once a day should be taken twice a day."

It didn't really matter to me either way. The way I thought of it was, what was one more prick? I was slowly learning to take everything I heard with a grain of salt. As time passed on the "Pity parties" were far and in between. Don't get me wrong; I still had them. They were great parties too with plenty tears, tissues, and "why me's"? Nevertheless, the little things no longer invited me to these parties.

Once while spending the day with a sick friend of mine, (she only had a cold,) I slowly became irritated with her complaints. Every five minutes it was "my throat hurts", "my nose is running", or the infamous "I just feel awful". I thought about the drunken feeling I get when my blood sugar was too low or the feverish way I felt when it was too high.

After one more complaint (the straw that broke the camel's back as my mother would say) I blurted out "Until your pancreas stops working SHUT UP!"

Sitting there with a frown on my face I glanced in her direction. She was beet red, shaking under the cover with tears of laughter flowing down her face. I started laughing also.

I officially had enough whining for the day so I left my friend to soak alone. When I arrived at my mother's house I told her about the events of my day. Like I assumed, she found the pancreas joke hilarious. The joke ended up leading to a conversation about God never putting on you more than you can bear. I am not the most religious person however, I am very spiritual (being the "Christian under construction" that I am). I agreed. I thought about some things I been through that many people I knew would not have handled well; and vice versa.

I was told a few weeks earlier that my pancreas doesn't work and I was essentially okay. Realistically speaking I told many a lot of my friends that I was diabetic because if I wasn't I would be fat and God knows that I can't take being fat. (Nothing against anyone heavier... I used to only date heavier men. But that's another story). Nevertheless, the conversation with my mother led me to the next great lesson I learned since diagnosis. Whining gets you nowhere.

My mother is the reason I fell in love with poetry. When I was a child she always gave lessons through proverbs, fables, and poetry. She encouraged me to write down my feelings instead of bottling them up as well as to talk about things. She would always "A closed mouth doesn't get fed." Most importantly when I would whine and complain about things going on she would recite her favorite poem by Langston Hughes and substitute the word "daughter" for son. Besides the life lesson that stuck with me I loved to watch her oratory displays. I can't be dishonest. There are many moments when I complain a little more than I should. But when my pancreas stopped working I learned to look at things a little differently.

Mother to Son by Langston Hughes

Well, son, I'll tell you:
Life for me ain't been no crystal stair.
It's had tacks in it,
And splinters,
And boards torn up,
And places with no carpet on the floor --
Bare.
But all the time
I'se been a-climbin' on,
And reachin' landin's,
And turnin' corners,
And sometimes goin' in the dark
Where there ain't been no light.
So boy, don't you turn back.
Don't you set down on the steps
'Cause you finds it's kinder hard.
Don't you fall now --
For I'se still goin', honey,
I'se still climbin',
And life for me ain't been no crystal stair.

Lesson #5: Whining gets you Nowhere; What happens afterwards takes you places

The bible says "When thou passest through the waters, I will be with thee; and through the rivers, they shall not overflow thee: when thou walkest through the fire, thou shalt not be burned; neither shall the flame kindle upon thee." – Isaiah 43:2-3 KJV

Whining about the matters of your life does two things: It gets you nowhere, and irritates those who are forced to listen. That's it. That doesn't mean that you don't deserve the opportunity to vent. Everyone does. But then what? It seems fairly easy to say that God never puts more on us than we can bear however, after the storm (plus reflection time) it becomes clear. It's a matter of us having the faith of a mustard seed to believe it and stand strong. After a while the tough skin is not something that is placed on like a coat. It is a natural permanent exterior layer. As if we were born with it.

CHAPTER 6: DIABETICS CAN'T GET TATTOOS? THEN WHY DO I HAVE SO MANY?

When I was a teenager I begged my mother for a tattoo. With a look worth 1000 words she stated, "You can get whatever you want when you get out my house." I knew that if I ever tried her and got one while I was still living in her house she just may try to black my eye. So I waited until I turned eighteen. On my birthday I got my first tattoo along with two of my best friends. I was not a diabetic at the time. By the time I found out I was a diabetic I had a total of three tattoos.

While watching a TV show about the art of tattooing one evening I learned why people believe diabetics should not get tattoos. A tattoo artist (who was also a type 1 diabetic) explained that if a person's glucose levels were not managed well it would take the tattoo longer to heal. Also, the pain from the process as well as the healing of the tattoo could cause unexpected drops in blood sugar. When I got my first tattoo as a diabetic I was extremely nervous. I checked my sugar a million times before arriving at the tattoo parlor. I couldn't bear to watch. When the tattoo was complete I stood in the mirror with admiration and concern. Would it heal normally? Would my glucose be an issue? For two weeks I monitored my sugar more than usual. The tattoo healed wonderfully.

Throughout the course of the years I got a total of thirteen tattoos in which three were cover ups. Nine of the tattoos were done in my diabetic life. I built great relationships with two primary tattoo artists who not only knew that I was a diabetic but who also knew I would be a stickler for glucose management even more whenever I got "inked". Still, no matter how many tattoos I have gotten (and continue to get) people would say "You shouldn't be getting tattoos as diabetic". If only some people would do their research before they opened their mouth to speak.

Tattooed people have their own culture; their own language. If I was unable to be a part of "my culture" due to my chronic disease I would have been devastated. As a diabetic woman I am able to be me. I am still able to eat sweets and I am still able to enjoy all the spoils of life. Most importantly my life isn't over.

Lesson #6: Learn the Value of Research

As a diabetic the most valuable lesson I have learned (that has continued to benefit me and my life in every way shape or form) is to do my own research. It is imperative to talk to your doctors, nurses, fellow diabetics, and to read books. Many people who think they know your disease don't have your disease. They don't understand what you have been through, what you go through, or the challenges to come. Diabetes and its treatments have evolved. On a sunny day last summer I enjoyed an ice cream cone with one of my friends. Her aunt came outside to join us.

"You can't eat ice cream, can you?"

I shrugged, "If I couldn't I am already huh?"

My friend and I giggled. Her aunt looked perplexed.

"You know, I read once that if you eat ice cream your blood sugar will rise and you will have to get your limbs cut off."

That was my red button. You know the button in the movies that they always tell people not to touch and when they do everything goes haywire? It seemed like a lot of people, especially older people, always found it convenient to talk about decapitation whenever they found out I was a T1D (type 1 diabetic). They told horror stories and more often than not implicated that losing a limb was inevitable in my future.

If I hadn't done my own research years prior and learned that usually when someone has a limb cut off if it was due to like 10 years of not monitoring their sugar, not taking their meds properly, and not making their health a top priority; I could have been more upset. If I hadn't done my own research and learned that people with type 2 diabetes are more prone to have a limb amputated than people with type

1; I could have been more upset. If I hadn't done my own research and discovered that many people who lose limbs lose them from peripheral vascular disease (not just because they are diabetic); I could have been more upset. But I wasn't because I did my research.

Instead of getting mad at the aura of ignorance that surrounded my friend's aunt I decided to poke fun.

"I already had my leg cut off. You know they are making prosthetics very real looking nowadays. So much so that I had mine tattooed. See?"

She believed me for a moment, then playfully hit me on my back.

Although I was bothered by her rude comment I laughed it off thinking about how knowledge is priceless. Research! Research! Research! The more you know the better equipped you are to deal with life and live your life to the fullest.

<u>Cessation</u>

Adjusting to life with diabetes is difficult. I would be nothing short of a liar if I said anything else. However, we are getting closer to a cure each day. Diabetes is not a death sentence. It does not define you as a person nor does it define your life. My great-grandfather would always say, "There is nothing wrong with getting old, its just inconvenient." He lived well into his 90's. Being a diabetic is inconvenient. The most important detail about being a diabetic is that if you take the take good care of yourself, you are already beating the disease.

PICTURES

A picture of my CGM (Continuous Glucose Monitor) the day my nurse helped me attach it.

This picture was taken a few months after I started working out with Zak

My biggest tattoo as a diabetic

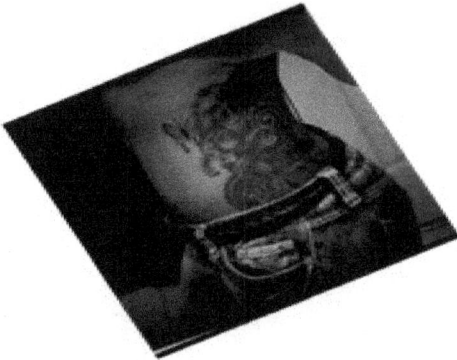

Shetoya T

Me and my mom at the
Walk to Cure diabetes
2010

FACTS

The Juvenile Diabetes Research Foundation (2011) provides the following facts about type 1 diabetes:

Fact Sheets: Type 1 Diabetes Facts
About T1D
Type 1 diabetes (T1D) is an autoimmune disease in which a person's pancreas stops producing insulin, a hormone that enables people to get energy from food. It occurs when the body's immune system attacks and destroys the insulin-producing cells in the pancreas, called beta cells. While its causes are not yet entirely understood, scientists believe that both genetic factors and environmental triggers are involved. Its onset has nothing to do with diet or lifestyle. There is nothing you can do to prevent T1D, and-at present-nothing you can do to get rid of it.
Affects Children and Adults
Type 1 diabetes strikes both children and adults at any age. It comes on suddenly, causes dependence on injected or pumped insulin for life, and carries the constant threat of devastating complications.
Needs Constant Attention
Living with T1D is a constant challenge. People with the disease must carefully balance insulin doses (either by injections multiple times a day or continuous infusion through a pump) with eating and daily activities throughout the day and night. They must also test their blood sugar by pricking their fingers for blood six or more times a day. Despite this constant attention, people with T1D still run the

risk of dangerous high or low blood sugar levels, both of which can be life-threatening. People with T1D overcome these challenges on a daily basis.

Not Cured By Insulin

While insulin injections or infusion allow a person with T1D to stay alive, they do not cure the disease, nor do they necessarily prevent the possibility of the disease's serious effects, which may include: kidney failure, blindness, nerve damage, amputations, heart attack, stroke, and pregnancy complications.

Perseverance and Hope

Although type 1 diabetes is a serious and difficult disease, treatment options are improving all the time, and people with T1D can lead full and active lives. JDRF is driving research to improve the technology people with T1D use to monitor blood sugar levels and deliver the proper doses of insulin, as well as research that will ultimately deliver a cure.

Statistics

• As many as three million Americans may have type 1 diabetes. 1

• Each year, more than 15,000 children and 15,000 adults - approximately 80 people per day - are diagnosed with type 1 diabetes in the U.S.2

• 85 percent of people living with type 1 diabetes are adults.3

• The rate of type 1 diabetes incidence among children under the age of 14 is estimated to increase by 3% annually worldwide. 4

Warning Signs

Warning signs of T1D may occur suddenly and include:

• Extreme thirst
• Frequent urination
• Drowsiness or lethargy
• Increased appetite
• Sudden weight loss
• Sudden vision changes
• Sugar in the urine

- Fruity odor on the breath
- Heavy or labored breathing
- Stupor or unconsciousness

What is it Like to Have T1D?

Ask people who have type 1 diabetes, and they will tell you: It's difficult. It's upsetting. It's life-threatening. It never goes away. But, at the same time, people with T1D serve as an inspiration by facing the disease's challenges with courage and perseverance and don't let it stand in the way of achieving their goals.

"Both children and adults like me who live with type 1 diabetes(T1D) need to be mathematicians, physicians, personal trainers, and dieticians all rolled into one. We need to be constantly factoring and adjusting, making frequent finger sticks to check blood sugars, and giving ourselves multiple daily insulin injections just to stay alive."

- JDRF International Chairman Mary Tyler Moore

"It is a 24/7/365 job. We never get to relax and forget about food, whether we've exercised too much or too little, insulin injections, blood sugar testing, or the impact of stress, a cold, a sunburn, and on and on. So many things make each day a risky venture when you live with T1D."

- Mary Vonnegut, adult, Rhode Island

"Unlike other kids, I have to check my blood sugar 8 to 10 times a day; everything I eat is measured and every carbohydrate counted. My kit goes with me everywhere I go.... Too much exercise or not eating all my food can be dangerous. I think I'm too young to have to worry about all this stuff."

- Jonathan Platt, 8, California

"It controls your life in ways that someone without it doesn't even see. For me, the worst part of living with T1D is the fear that my three children or their children might develop the disease."

- Nicky Hider, adult, New York

1 Type 1 Diabetes, 2010; Prime Group for JDRF, Mar. 2011

2   NIDDK:
http://diabetes.niddk.nih.gov/dm/pubs/statistics/index.htm#i_youn
gpeople
   3 Type 1 Diabetes, 2010; Prime Group for JDRF, Mar. 2011
   4   IDF: http://www.idf.org/diabetesatlas/diabetes-young-global-
perspective

REFERENCES

(2012). *tattoo gun.* (2012). [Print Photo]. Retrieved from http://www.squidoo.com/Printable_tribal_tattoo_designs.

(2011). birthday cake clipart. (2011). [Web Photo]. Retrieved from http://clip-art-free-clipart.blogspot.com/2009/11/birthday-cake-clipart.html

(2011). irg woman silhouette. (2011). [Web Photo]. Retrieved from http://cliparts101.com/free_clipart/5429/Woman_Silhouette_36.aspx

American diabetes association and jdrf. (2010, December). Retrieved from http://www.jdrf.org/index.cfm?page_id=102585

Carbohydrate counting 101. In (2011). Joslin Diabetes Center Retrieved from http://www.joslin.org/info/Carbohydrate_Counting_101.html

(n.d.). man with diabetes giving himself an insulin shot. [Web Photo]. Retrieved from http://www.best-of-web.com/pages/101108-201860-946042.html

(n.d.). Obese silhouette. [Web Photo]. Retrieved from http://stockpicturesforeveryone.blogspot.com/2011/02/obesity-silhouettes.html

(n.d.). Retrieved from http://clipart-for-free.blogspot.com/2008/09/free-exercise-clipart.html

Sattley, M. (2008, December 17). Diabetes health. Retrieved from htt p://www.diabeteshealth.com/read/2008/12/17/715/the-history-of-diabetes/

ABOUT THE AUTHOR

The Chicago native, Shetoya T., is the author of *Ballad of the Ghetto Child: Bailey's Song*. As a student at Morgan Park High School she dreamed of the day that she would see her name on a book. After graduating from the University of Missouri-Columbia she took time to focus on helping others as a housing case manager, while her literary dreams took a temporary back seat. However, she breathed, ate, and slept with "ink" on her mind. Now, at the age of 26, she watches her dreams come to life in front of her own eyes. While she enjoys writing fiction her urge to complete an informational and educational memoir about her battle with type 1 diabetes could not be resisted. After being diagnosed shortly after her 21st birthday she learned to live a "sweet" life. *You Got the Sugar?* tells exactly how she did so.

www.ingramcontent.com/pod-product-compliance
Lightning Source LLC
Chambersburg PA
CBHW061757040426
42447CB00011B/2347